# Fine Art Studio
# Painting

## by Mary Iverson

# For Julia

## Silver Dolphin

Silver Dolphin Books
An imprint of the Advantage Publishers Group
5880 Oberlin Drive, San Diego, CA 92121-4794
www.silverdolphinbooks.com

Text copyright © 2004 by becker&mayer!

*Fine Art Studio: Painting* is produced by becker&mayer!,
Bellevue, Washington
www.beckermayer.com

If you have questions or comments about this product, send e-mail to
infobm@beckermayer.com

ISBN-13 : 978-1-59223-328-1
ISBN-10 : 1-59223-328-7

Produced, manufactured, and assembled in China.

3 4 5 09 08 07 06 05

05348

Edited by Ben Grossblatt
Written & Illustrated by Mary Iverson
Designed by J. Max Steinmetz
Design assistance by Karrie Lee
Packaging design by Scott Westgard
Studio photography by Keith Megay
Product development by Lillis Taylor
Production management by Katie Stephens

Special thanks to the artists who contributed paintings to this book:
Pirjo Berg, Andrée Carter, Chuck Close, Stephanie Dennis, Michael
Dickter, Carole D'Inverno, Helen Frankenthaler, Patricia Hagen, Virginia
Howlett, Randy McCoy, Joanne Pavlak, Aaron Power, and Sandra
Power.

### Image Credits

Every effort has been made to correctly attribute all the material
reproduced in this book. We will be happy to correct any errors in
future editions.

**Page 3:** The "Chinese Horse" (prehistoric cave painting), Lascaux
Caves, Perigord, Dordogne, France, photo: Art Resource, NY.
**Page 10:** Henri Matisse, *Vegetative Elements* © Succession H.
Matisse, Paris / Artists Rights Society (ARS), New York, photo: Jens
Ziehe, Bildarchiv Preussischer Kulturbesitz / Art Resource, NY.
**Page 15:** Sandra Power, *After Lunch* and *Granny's Apples,* photos:
Richard Nicol.
**Page 16:** Claude Monet, *Waterlily Pond, Harmony in Pink,*
photo: Erich Lessing / Art Resource, NY.

**Page 20:** Georges Seurat, *Port-en-Bassin, Outer Harbor at High Tide,*
photo: Erich Lessing / Art Resource, NY.
**Page 23:** Randy McCoy, *Joshua Trees* and Stephanie Dennis,
*Waterfall,* photos: Richard Nicol.
**Page 24:** Chuck Close, *Kiki* © Chuck Close, photo: Walker Art
Center.
**Pages 28–29:** Laughing children © Tom Grill/CORBIS, used with
permission.
**Page 31:** Sandra Power, *Artist with Red Flowers* and Carole
D'Inverno, Untitled, photos: Richard Nicol.
**Page 32:** Helen Frankenthaler, *Acres,* photo: ESM—Ed Meneely / Art
Resource, NY.
**Page 37:** Stephanie Dennis, *Turquoise,* Joanne Pavlak, Untitled, and
Randy McCoy, Untitled, photos: Richard Nicol.
**Page 38:** Rhino (prehistoric cave painting), photo: Jean Clottes,
document elaborated with the support of the French Ministry
of Culture and Communication, Regional Direction for Cultural
Affairs—Rhône-Alpes, Regional Department of Archaeology;
Leonardo da Vinci, *Mona Lisa,* photo: Scala / Art Resource, NY.
**Page 39:** Pablo Picasso, *Portrait of Dora Maar* © 2004 Estate of
Pablo Picasso / Artists Rights Society (ARS), New York, photo:
Réunion des Musées Nationaux / Art Resource, NY; Jackson Pollock,
*Watery Paths* © 2004 The Pollock-Krasner Foundation / Artists
Rights Society (ARS), New York, photo: Bridgeman-Giraudon /
Art Resource, NY; Chuck Close, *Robert/104,072* © Chuck Close,
courtesy of PaceWildenstein, New York.

# The Power of Painting

On a September day, on a hill overlooking the village of Montignac, France, four boys race through a sun-scorched meadow, chasing their dog, Robot. When they catch up to him, Robot is sniffing at the ground beside an uprooted pine tree, barking and wagging his tail suspiciously. There's a hole in the ground! The boys lead Robot home, but can't get that hole out of their minds. A few days later they return with ropes and homemade lanterns. They lower themselves down, their lanterns casting a dim glow on the ground far below. Finally, they reach the bottom. They've discovered the entrance to a vast cavern! They lift their lanterns and see lions, bison, and deer leap to life! A rhinoceros gallops right in front of their faces!

The boys have made one of the most incredible discoveries of all time: the cave paintings at Lascaux, the grandest of prehistoric underground galleries. The paintings are more than 15,000 years old, and stretch along an intricate network of caverns. They've been preserved all this time, unseen, waiting to be discovered.

The cave paintings are a great example of painting's power to convey the human experience. We all have an undeniable need to communicate, to explain ideas, to express feelings. The prehistoric artists did all this through their painting, creating images that could inspire people thousands of years later.

*Paintings like this—made thousands and thousands of years ago when someone spat "paint" onto his hand—reveal that painting isn't just about technique or skill with a brush. It's also about the need to say "I am here!"*

# Table of Contents

# Brushes & Materials

Your painting
kit includes:
Palette
Palette knife
4 canvases
3 paintbrushes
2 transparent grids
7 tubes of acrylic paint
1 sheet of heavy paper

## Brushes

The parts of a paintbrush are the bristles, the ferrule (a metal piece that holds the bristles together), and the handle. Until the middle of the 19th century, artists made their own brushes in the studio from animal hair, wood, and metal.

While some modern brushes are still crafted from natural materials, many are made from synthetic fibers and plastic. These brushes can be more durable and are often less expensive than brushes made from the hair of a sable. Synthetic sable brushes are ideal for acrylics because they are durable yet soft.

In your kit you have two types of brushes: a flat and two rounds.

Handle
Ferrule
Bristles

### Expensive Art Supplies

The most expensive brushes in the world are made from kolinsky sable, which is hair taken from the tails of Siberian minks.

## Caring for your brushes

By taking a little bit of time to take care of your brushes after each painting session, you can ensure that they will last a long time.

1) As soon as you finish using them, clean your brushes with liquid dish soap and warm water. Squirt a little dish soap into the palm of your hand. Rub the bristles into the soap. Rinse and repeat until there's no paint in the soap suds.

2) Never let paint dry on the brush. This is especially important with acrylic paint, because when it dries on a brush, it becomes hard, like plastic, and is almost impossible to remove.

3) Don't leave a brush sitting in a water jar for long periods of time, especially if it is resting on its bristles. This will cause the bristles to permanently bend. The handle may also crack if it becomes saturated with water.

## Palette Knife

Your palette knife can be used to mix paints, apply paint to the canvas, make marks in the paint, scrape paint off the canvas, or clean paint off a palette.

Blade

Handle

## Palette

A palette is any surface on which paint can be mixed. In your kit, your palette is made of plastic. It has a mixing surface and walls to keep paint and water from spilling out.

## Cleaning Your Palette

Acrylic paints are easy to remove from metal, glass, ceramic, or plastic. Once the paint is dry, just peel or scrape it off with your palette knife. You can use warm, soapy water to remove any remaining paint.

*Recycled plastic containers can be used if you need extra palettes.*

*For a bigger mixing area, you could use an old plate, lid, or even an ice cube tray.*

## Paint

Paint comes in limitless colors, many of which have strange and exotic names such as lapis, carmine, and burnt sienna. These names all relate to the source of the *pigment* used to make the paint. Pigment is a fine, dustlike powder. Lapis lazuli is a dazzling blue gemstone—when it's ground up it makes the blue pigment in lapis. Carmine is the name of a brilliant red pigment derived from beetle shells. Burnt sienna is a brown pigment made by grinding up rocks from Sienna, a city in Italy.

To make paint, pigments are mixed with a thick fluid called a *binder*. In oil paint, the binder is linseed oil. Watercolors are made with gum arabic, a saplike substance that comes from the African acacia tree. The binder in acrylic paint, the paint you have in your kit, is called polymer emulsion, which is a substance similar to white glue.

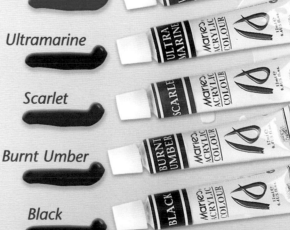

Titanium White

Lemon Yellow

Viridian

Ultramarine

Scarlet

Burnt Umber

Black

*If you run out of paint, you can buy more at any art supply store. Remember to get acrylics!*

# The Color Wheel

What would a painting be without color? It is impossible to talk about painting without talking about color, because paintings are built with color. Color is what makes painting special.

Some painters use a wide array of colors, while others choose to paint with very few.

Have you ever heard the phrase "show your true colors"? That means "show the real you." By making a painting, you are doing exactly that—expressing what you have inside.

The *color wheel* is a tool for seeing and describing relationships between colors.

Learning the arrangement of colors on the color wheel can help you to mix colors (and think about colors) like a real painter.

The color wheel consists of 12 colors: three primary colors, three secondary colors, and six tertiary (TUR-she-airy), or "third-level," colors.

*Color Wheel*

*Primary Colors*

*Secondary Colors*

*Tertiary Colors*

## Primary Colors

Red, yellow, and blue are the three *primary colors*. These colors are also called *foundation colors* because they are used to create all other colors. They can't be created by mixing any other colors. (If a painting kit doesn't include red, yellow, and blue, you're out of luck. There's no way to make primary colors on your own.)

## Secondary Colors

Orange, green, and violet are the three *secondary colors*. Each one is formed by combining two primary colors. Mixing red and yellow together makes orange, mixing blue and yellow makes green, and mixing red and blue makes violet.

## Tertiary Colors

The six *tertiary colors* are made by combining a primary and a neighboring secondary color. The tertiary colors are red-orange, yellow-orange, yellow-green, blue-green, blue-violet, and red-violet.

## Warm and Cool Colors

Blue, and colors that contain a predominance of blue (such as green and violet) are considered *cool colors*.

Red, yellow, orange, and red-violet are considered *warm colors*

There is no absolute cutoff between the warm and cool colors. A color's context can make it seem warmer or cooler. For example, light green could be a warm color when placed next to dark blue, but appear cooler when placed next to orange.

*Cool Colors*

*Warm Colors*

*Neutral Colors*

## Complementary Colors

Any two colors that sit directly across from each other on the color wheel are called *complementary colors*

Complementary Colors

## Neutral Colors

When two complementary colors are mixed together, they make a *neutral*. Grays, browns, and earth tones are examples of neutrals.

# Techniques

Brushstrokes can be bold and rhythmic, choppy and faceted, or smoothly blended.

The way an artist uses the brush can make a big difference in the character of a painting.

**Flat:** This large brush carries a lot of paint. It can be used for blocking in broad areas of color. Brushstrokes made with a flat have angular edges.

**Round:** The smaller round brushes are best for detail work and for creating brushstrokes with soft, curved edges.

Each brush makes a different mark. Because the flat brush is large, it's the best one for painting a broad area, such as a sky. The medium-sized round will probably be your most-used brush. It's good for almost anything. Your smallest brush makes tiny marks and is great for details (and for signing your name to your work).

Try using all of your brushes and any color of paint. Experiment with the different types of marks you can make.

## How to Mix Paint

Start with small blobs of paint on your palette. Use your palette knife and pick up a little bit of one color and add it to a blob of another color. Blend the colors together by pressing the blade of the palette knife into the paint. Move the blade a little and press again, smearing the colors together. Keep doing this—adding more color if necessary—until the mix looks just right. You can also mix acrylic paints with a brush.

## TOOLS OF THE TRADE

### Brush Tips

1. Hold your brush loosely, like a pencil, or any way that's comfortable.
2. Dip your brush in water before you dip it in the paint. This helps the paint to flow off of the brush.
3. Rinse off your brush between colors: Swish it vigorously in the water and press the bristles against the bottom of your water jar. Check the brush. Have you rinsed all the color off?

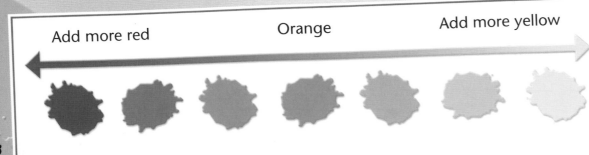

Add more red     Orange     Add more yellow

Practice your mixing technique by blending different amounts of red and yellow to create a range of oranges.

## Tints & Shades

*Tint* is the name for a pastel-like version of a color, made by adding white. You might use a tint when painting a bright, sunny landscape.

Adding black to any color makes a *shade*. Shades can be used to paint shadows or nighttime scenes.

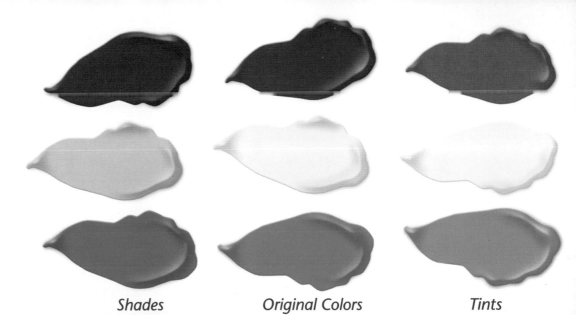

Shades · Original Colors · Tints

| Color | Tint | Shade | Neutral | Gray |
|---|---|---|---|---|

*A color chart can help you get a feel for your paints and how they work together to make tints, shades, neutrals, and grays.*

## Exercise: Color Chart

When painters get a new set of paints, they like to do mixing experiments with them before making any paintings. All paints are different. It's a good idea to get to know your paints and how they feel and mix.

Draw a grid with five columns and five rows. (That's one row for each color in your kit, not including white, black, and brown—and orange. You'll have to mix the orange yourself.)

## Acrylics Dry Fast

To keep your acrylic paints from drying, remember these important steps whenever you paint:

1. Clean off your palette knife with a paper towel between each color you mix.

2. Put the caps back on your tubes right after you squeeze out the paint.

3. Spray your palette with water from a spray bottle after you squeeze out the paint. Repeat this often while you are painting or mixing colors to keep it from drying on the palette.

Now that you're beginning to get a feel for your brushes and paints, it's time to jump into the first painting project.

# Still Lifes

A still life painting is a composition of objects such as fruit, flowers, dishes, books, or musical instruments.

Still life is a tradition of painting seen as early as the first century BC, when Roman artists painted decorative murals on the plaster walls of their houses. The definition of still life painting has evolved since then, expanding from a style of decoration to an arena for expressing feelings, showing off an artist's painting technique, presenting new ideas about art, or telling stories through the arrangement of symbolic objects.

The best still life paintings are more than just pictures of objects. The choice of objects can tell a story. For example, an artist could use a still life painting to talk about a friend. The arranged items might include a candle to represent that person's intelligence, a lemon to describe their zest for life, a tree branch to mark a love of the outdoors, and a violin to show their interest in music.

Henri Matisse, Vegetative Elements, 1947.
Cutout gouache on paper on linen, 65 x 50 cm.
Nationalgalerie, Museum Berggruen,
Staatliche Museen zu Berlin, Berlin, Germany.

## Henri Matisse, the Poet of Color

Henri Matisse (1869–1954) was a much-loved artist and a master of the still life. His paintings were celebrations of color.

While confined to bed for months after an appendectomy, Matisse began drawing to pass the time, and he discovered his artistic talent. Soon after that, he quit his job and moved to Paris to study art.

He declared that the purpose of art was to produce pleasing, soothing images, "something like a good armchair which provides relaxation for physical fatigue." He was called "the poet of color" because of the way his paintings used color to reveal the essence of beauty in a way that everyone could understand.

In 1946, when Matisse was 72 years old, his eyesight deteriorated, which made it difficult for him to work on paintings with any kind of detail. This setback did not stop him from working. Always the innovator, he came up with a way of working that accommodated his ailment. With a pair of scissors and sheets of brightly painted paper, he crafted *collages*, arrangements of materials with different shapes and colors, which became his most memorable works.

## Materials

You will need the following materials (in addition to your kit's paints, brushes, sheet of heavy paper, palette, and palette knife):

- Jars (mayonnaise jars and peanut butter jars work well—rinse them out thoroughly and don't forget the lids)
- Paper or board to glue the collage onto
- White drawing paper
- More heavy paper (optional)
- Plain white glue
- Paper towels
- Spray bottle
- Glue stick
- Scissors
- Pencil

# Painting a Still Life Collage

Your first project is a Matisse-inspired still life. You'll create a sketch, cut out shapes, and arrange them into a colorful collage.

**EXAMPLE OF A STILL LIFE**

## 1 Arrange Your Still Life

The subject matter of still lifes has usually fallen into a few basic categories, including flowers in a vase, fruit in a bowl, food on a table, and other arrangements of familiar items. You could survey your home for items that are pleasing and brightly colored, or anything with an interesting shape.

Or you could create a theme of your own and choose a group of related items that reflect your idea. For example, you might choose to work with the color red, arranging a variety of red objects on a crimson tablecloth.

In this example, a bowl of fruit is perfect because the colors are bright and the shapes are simple and familiar.

Re-create it with fruit in a bowl on a solid-color tablecloth. Push the table against a wall that is a solid color.

### Other Still Life Inspirations

Winter
The beach
Your best friend
Your favorite subject in school

Can you think of a way to represent these themes and turn them into still lifes, using an arrangement of objects?

*Painting Secrets: Composition*
To create a composition that works, arrange the objects in your still life inside an imaginary triangle or circle.

## 2 Make a Preparatory Sketch

To begin, make a sketch of your still life on a piece of paper. In your sketch, simplify the outlines of the various shapes. You will be cutting these out with scissors, so basic shapes are best. Fill the whole sheet of paper with your drawing, allowing some of the shapes to touch the edges.

Instead of striving for an exact replica of your still life, you could allow some shapes to dance in the drawing by moving them around or by tilting them a little bit.

*A sample still life arrangement*

## 3 Prepare the Surface

First, you will need to prepare your paper by painting the back with *glue sizing*. Glue sizing will help to keep the paper from curling when you paint the colors on the front side.

Spread a thin coat of sizing onto your paper. Allow the sizing to dry before applying colors.

When it's dry, cut the paper into squares.

*Be sure to spread the gesso evenly—a little bit goes a long way.*

## TOOLS OF THE TRADE

You can buy sizing, called *gesso* (JESS-oh), in any art supply store. Or you can make your own. To make glue sizing, mix four parts white glue and one part water in a jar. Stir with your palette knife.

## 4 Working with Color (Yellow, Green, and Black)

Now it's time to mix your colors and paint the pieces of paper for the collage. What are the main colors in your still life? In our bowl-of-fruit example, we have red, yellow, orange, green, blue, and black.

For yellow, green, and black, paint each square of paper a solid color. Apply the paint to the side of the paper without the gesso on it. Work with one color at a time, cleaning your brush and wiping off your palette between colors. To get a solid color on your paper, apply two coats of paint. Allow the paint to dry between coats.

## 5 Making Tints of Red and Blue

Two of the colors in your kit, blue and red, are transparent. This means the colors might not look rich and deep when you paint with them.

To take care of this, mix a little bit of white paint into the colors to create tints of them. When your tint looks just the way you want, spread it onto one of your squares of paper. Dip the widest brush into the water and then spread an even coat onto a square of paper. When the paint is dry, apply a second coat.

*Paint the side without the gesso.*

### Painting Secrets: Warm Tints

Sometimes, adding white to a color cools it down, making it look lifeless and even a little on the blue side. To offset this, add a spot of yellow to the mix for warmth. Can you see the difference?

Pure red          Red tint          Red tint warmed up with yellow

## 6 Mixing Orange

Squeeze some red and yellow paint onto your palette in equal amounts. Now mix a tiny dab of red into the yellow to make a yellow-orange. Continue adding red, bit by bit, until you have the orange that you like. Paint it onto another square of heavy paper.

*Add red to yellow, bit by bit, to make orange.*

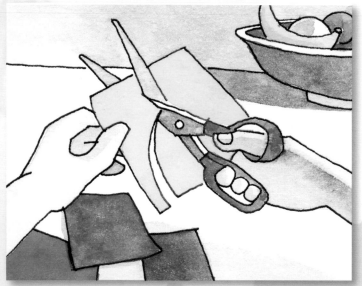

Using your sketch as a guide, cut out shapes from your painted squares of paper to represent the fruit, the bowl, and the table.

Think about the shapes you see in your sketch. Look at Matisse's collage for inspiration. He liked to use overlapping pieces and even small scraps. The shapes he used weren't perfectly recognizable, but the painting feels like leaves and plants just the same.

Arrange the shapes on a board or piece of heavy paper.

When you find an arrangement that you like, use the glue stick to glue each piece onto the board. You may want to add additional shapes for texture and pattern.

## The Finished Still Life

## More Still Life Projects to Try:

- *Books on a bookshelf*
- *Flowers in a vase*
- *The table and chairs in your dining room*
- *Shoes and socks*
- *Sports equipment*

## Other Approaches to Still Lifes

Matisse's collage technique is only one way of making a still life. The following examples feature techniques ranging from super-realism to near abstraction, and give you an idea of the ways painters can play with still lifes.

Sandra Power, *After Lunch*, 2004.
Oil on canvas, 12 x 9 in.

Michael Dickter, *Goldfish*, 2004.
Oil on canvas, 12 x 12 in.

Still life paintings can be based on another painter's work. Michael Dickter based this piece on a painting of a goldfish bowl done by Matisse. This painting is almost abstract, but we can still recognize the shapes and colors of the goldfish.

A still life doesn't have to show things we usually think of as beautiful. This still life is a thoughtful, balanced setup of the garbage left over from lunch. With the right composition and technique, even this can make for a beautiful still life.

Sandra Power, *Granny's Apples*, 2003.
Oil on canvas, 18 x 24 in.

Randy McCoy, *Martha and I*, 2002.
Oil on canvas, 72 x 92 in.

This painter chooses bold colors, as Matisse did in his still life collages, but here they are applied with loose, lively brushstrokes. This still life features a bouquet of flowers in front of a boldly striped, abstract background. The artist, Randy McCoy, uses the stripe motif in many of his paintings as a signature style.

Sandra Power paints in a realistic style with an incredible amount of precision and detail. This still life focuses on the bright green of a bunch of Granny Smith apples. She balances the green with notes of red (the complement of green) in the handles of the kitchen implements. The objects in the still life have a variety of surfaces, from soft, textured cloth to smooth, reflective metal and shiny apples. Power's ability to show the differences between all of these textures demonstrates her great skill.

15

# Landscapes

Landscape painting is the art of depicting scenery in painting. The idea of landscape painting can stretch to include nearly anything. While some landscape painters paint pictures of trees and wildflowers, others feature buildings and urban landscapes in their paintings. What kinds of things in your everyday life could be considered landscape?

## Impressionism

In the late 1800s, a new style of painting arose in France. It was called Impressionism, and painters who painted in this style created landscapes like no one had ever seen. The goal of the Impressionists (including Monet, Renoir, Cezanne, Degas, and Manet) was to capture the light and color they saw in the natural world. They produced sparkling paintings full of shimmering color.

## Technological Innovations

Before the Impressionists came along, artists had been mainly interested in painting as realistically as possible. The introduction of photography in 1870 changed all that. Because cameras were better than any painter at producing realistic images, painters were free to experiment with new styles and techniques.

Another factor that influenced the Impressionists was the invention of tube paints in 1840. Before that, artists made their own paints using a time-consuming process. Tube paints were portable, practical, and convenient. Artists could go out and buy them! The time an artist used to spend in his studio grinding pigments could now be spent outside, painting.

### The right way to say it

| | |
|---|---|
| Monet | mo-NAY |
| Renoir | ren-WA |
| Cezanne | say-ZAN |
| Degas | day-GA |
| Manet | ma-NAY |

Claude Monet, *Waterlily Pond, Harmony in Pink*, 1900. Oil on canvas, 89.5 x 100 cm. Musée d'Orsay, Paris, France.

## Claude Monet, the Man in the Garden

One of the gardeners of Claude Monet (1840–1926) worked full-time maintaining the lily pond on the grounds of his large garden. Every day, dust stirred up by cars driving along a nearby dirt road settled onto the leaves of the water lilies, leaving them looking dull and lifeless. But Monet needed them to shine so that he could capture the bright green reflections in his paintings. To solve this problem, he asked his gardener to clean off the lily pads every day so that they would be perfect for Monet's morning painting session. The gardener got up at three o'clock in the morning and rowed his boat around the pond, wiping the dust off of hundreds of floating leaves!

## Materials

You will need the following materials (in addition to your kit's paints, brushes, palette, palette knife, and canvas):

- White drawing paper
- Paper towels
- Jar for water
- Spray bottle
- Pencil

# Creating an Impressionist Landscape

By applying paint the way Monet and the other Impressionists did—laying down countless small strokes of specially mixed colors—you will paint a shimmering portrait of nature.

## 1 Choose Your Subject

Landscape paintings can include subjects as vast as a wide, sun-drenched vista or as small as a single flower in a garden. The only limitation is that the subject matter be outside. It's the out-of-doors aspect that makes it a landscape painting.

When choosing what to include in your painting, try to keep things as simple as possible. For example, if you were going to paint a picture of your backyard, you might want to narrow it down to a small area of the yard, like the corner with the birdbath or the rose bushes, or a bench in the sunshine. It is easy to get overwhelmed in the landscape because there is so much to see all around us.

When Monet painted in his garden, he focused on one area at a time. Some days he would paint his water lilies. Other days he might look at a pathway edged with trees, or focus on just one particular flower.

CHOOSE SOMETHING THAT APPEALS TO YOU, AS IT WILL HELP YOU TO MAINTAIN YOUR INTEREST.

## 2 Make a Simple Sketch

In this example, the landscape is complex, with lots of details, colors, and trees and bushes. There is so much to look at in the photograph that it would be a good idea to narrow down the view and focus on some strong, simple shapes.

Thumbnail sketches are a valuable tool to help you do this. They got their name from being so small, like the nail of your thumb.

When you find a landscape idea that you feel like painting, sit down and do several thumbnails of your own, experimenting with a variety of framings.

# 3 Move to the Canvas

The next step is to copy this sketch, in pencil, on your canvas. Remember, this sketch is just a guideline for you to use when you begin to work with color. Don't spend a lot of time getting the sketch exactly right. Use very little detail—just enough to give yourself a general idea of what goes where.

From our thumbnails, it looks like the close-up of the azalea bush would make the best painting. This is how a quick sketch on the canvas would look.

## You're the Boss

When you paint, you're the boss. This means that you can omit or include any part of the landscape you like. In this example, there are some things left out that were there in the photograph. The rock, the yellow sprig of grass, and the background buildings were removed. This is called using your *artistic license*. Remember, you're creating an artistic version of part of the real world, not taking a photograph of it.

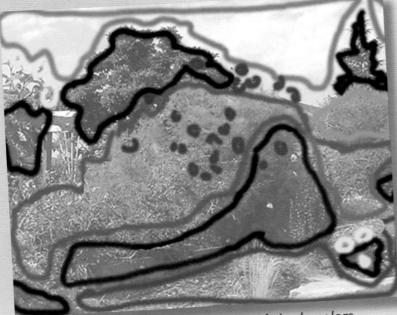

A color map shows large areas of single colors.

# 4 Create a Color Map

The landscape includes infinite colors. To get started on your painting, narrow those colors down to just a few. Our example can be broken down into five basic colors: sky blue, pink, brown, and green. Green in this example comes in three varieties: bright green for the bush, blue-green for the tree in the background and for the shadows of the bush, and yellow-green for the bright areas of the bush.

Lightly draw outlines around the areas where each color is found. Don't worry about putting in a lot of detail. This color map is just to help you get started.

## Mix Like Monet

The colors you mix for an Impressionist landscape don't need to be completely blended. Leaving in unmixed streaks of color when you mix paints on your palette can create the kind of color variation Impressionists love.

## 5 Add the First Colors

Our composition can be broken down into seven basic colors: sky blue, sunflower yellow, pink, brown, and three varieties of green.

**Sky Blue:** Mix one big dot of white plus a small dot of blue.

**Sunflower Yellow:** Use color right from the tube.

**Pink:** Mix one big dot of white plus a small dot of red.

**Brown:** Mix one small dot each of red, blue, and yellow.

## Mixing Greens

Landscape paintings are often filled with a wide spectrum of greens. For our example, we will need to create three different greens:

**Bright Green:** Mix one big dot each of green and yellow.

**Yellow-green:** Mix one big dot of yellow plus a small dot of green.

**Blue-green:** Mix one big dot each of green and blue.

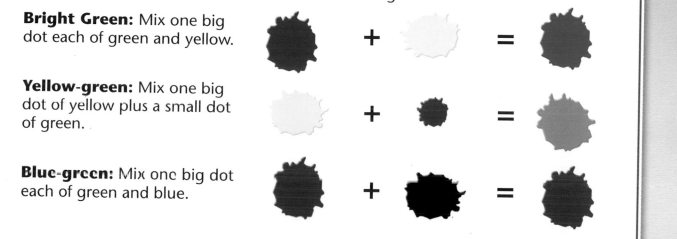

## Beginning to Paint

Although a finished Impressionist painting has hundreds of colors in it, all of them next to each other in a field of brushstrokes, it begins with a limited number of brushstrokes and just a few colors.

In the early stages of your painting, apply your colors to the canvas with your flat brush in small, loose brushstrokes. Leave plenty of space between brushstrokes for the variations of the colors that you will be mixing next.

## Advanced Concept: Optical Mixing

Traditionally, artists mix colors on a palette before applying them to the canvas. For example, you would create yellow-orange by mixing yellow and orange on a palette. Impressionists used a different technique called *optical mixing*. This involves painting the colors next to each other on the canvas, unmixed. Instead of using blended colors, optical mixing lets your eyes do the mixing. The Impressionists believed optical mixing resulted in more intense hues, re-creating the vibrating quality of light and giving the viewer an experience of sparkling sunlight.

*In this painting by Georges Seurat, all those tiny points of paint make the hills look alive and lush. The water sparkles and the sky has depth. Even the sailboats are made of little dots!*

Georges Seurat, *Port-en-Bessin, Outer Harbor at High Tide,* 1888. Oil on canvas, 67 x 82 cm. Musée d'Orsay, Paris, France.

## Pointillism

Optical mixing was a trademark of the painters of the Pointillism (POINT-uh-lizm) movement of the late 19th and early 20th centuries. These artists, among them Seurat, Signac, and Dubois-Pillet, created images made of tiny dots of paint. Seen close up, these dots are just colorful spots. But when you see a pointillist painting from farther away, the dots disappear and you see the painting's subject in colors that practically twinkle.

## Brush Tips

1. Use your medium-sized round brush for most of this painting. You could use the flat for part of the sky and path, but Impressionists generally use a round. Save your tiny brush for adding small flowers and details.

2. Impressionists use lots of paint. After you mix your colors, load your brush up and make short, thick strokes with it.

## 6 Color Variations

In an Impressionist landscape, there are hundreds of colors and more brushstrokes than you can count.

Mix color variations and apply them to your canvas in the spaces between your first brushstrokes.

Apply these colors to your canvas with your larger round brush.

### Variations of Sky Blue

Mix a big dot of white, a small dot of blue, and a small dot of yellow.

Mix a big dot of white, a small dot of yellow, and a speck of red (just enough red to cover the tip of your brush).

### Variations of Sunflower Yellow

Mix a big dot of white and a big dot of yellow.

Mix a big dot of white, a big dot of yellow, and a small dot of red.

### Variations of Pink

Mix a big dot of white, a small dot of red, and a small dot of yellow.

Mix a big dot of white, a small dot of yellow, and a speck of red.

### Variation of Brown

Mix a big dot each of red, brown, yellow, and white.

### Variations of Bright Green

Mix a big dot of yellow and a small dot of blue.

Mix a big dot of white, two big dots of yellow, a small dot of red, and a small dot of green.

### Variations of Yellow-green

Mix a big dot of yellow and a tiny dot of green.

Mix a big dot of white, a big dot of yellow, and a small dot of green.

### Variations of Blue-green

Mix a big dot of blue, a big dot of green, and a medium dot of white.

Mix a big dot of green and a big dot of yellow.

# 7 Mixing Color Variations for Depth

Some objects in the landscape are close, while others, like a distant hillside, are farther away. The next set of colors we will be mixing can build this depth into your painting.

To bring depth into your painting, mix variations of your first colors that are cool or neutral. You can mix these variations by adding blue, white, or your color's complement to the first colors that you used.

## Advanced Concept: Atmospheric Perspective

To show this depth in your painting, you need to employ *atmospheric perspective*. This is a system of color used to describe objects as they move into the distance.

There are three rules of atmospheric perspective that you need to know as a painter:

1. Warm colors advance and cool colors recede.
2. Objects in the distance appear lighter.
3. Colors in the distance are more neutral than colors seen close up.

## Final Variations for Richness and Depth

**Add to the lower part of the sky:**

a big dot of white, a small dot of yellow, and a tiny dot of blue.

**Add to the distant trees to push them further into the distance:**

a small dot each of blue, yellow, and white.

**Add to the front bushes:**

a big dot of green and two big dots of yellow.

**Add to the shadows below the bushes and on the path:**

a big dot of blue, two small dots of red, and two small dots of yellow.

Apply brushstrokes of these new variations to your canvas, next to the colors you've already applied.

Also, intersperse some of the new colors into other areas of the canvas, among the other colors. This will help to give a unified feeling to the painting.

Continue adding color variations until your canvas is covered.

## The Finished Landscape

## Other Approaches to Landscape Painting

There are many other ways to approach landscape painting. Instead of taking a Monet-like approach, you could create any kind of landscape you can imagine: bold and bright, moody, realistic, or quick and sketchy. Here are some examples of landscapes.

This painting of Joshua trees shows another type of landscape. The artist uses an almost cartoonlike style to depict the trees, a house, and a path. This simple treatment of shapes, along with the bold stripes in the background, creates a lively, fun feeling in the painting.

Randy McCoy, *Joshua Trees*, 2004.
Oil on canvas, 40 x 55 in.

This landscape is on the verge of abstraction. Because there is so little in the painting that is definite or recognizable, it leaves the story open for the viewer to interpret. What do you see in the painting? Do you see a hillside? Do you think the pale stripe is a tall tree? A waterfall? The painting has a mysterious, dreamy quality. The artist uses a narrow range of colors and knits them together with a network of loose brushstrokes. The result is a field of dark, rosy tones that give the feeling of calmness, making the viewer want to sit back and allow the colors to sink in.

Stephanie Dennis, *Waterfall*, 2003.
Oil on canvas, 60 x 80 in.

Like Monet, this artist likes to narrow the focus and concentrate on a small part of the landscape, in this case one special tree. He applied the paint in multiple layers, using loose brushstrokes.

Between each application of color, the artist has allowed the paint to dry. You can see the older colors peeking through gaps in newer layers of paint. This layering effect gives the feeling of weathering, as if the painting has stood for a very long time, like a tree.

You may have noticed that across the top of the canvas, the artist wrote the word *sequence*. He often uses words in his paintings to suggest different meanings. In this case, the word might refer to the passage of time in a tree's life, or to the many layers of paint on the canvas.

Michael Dickter, *One Tree*, 2002.
Oil on canvas, 48 x 34 in.

*More Landscape Projects to Try:*

- *The front of your house*
- *A wooden fence*
- *The beach*
- *A park*
- *A landmark in your neighborhood*

23

# Portraits

Your face speaks volumes about who you are. For centuries, artists have used painting to describe themselves and to share how others look. A portrait is a painted likeness of a person. A self-portrait is a painted likeness that an artist makes of himself or herself.

## Photorealism

Chuck Close is a well-known portrait artist who employs a style called *photorealism* to paint his larger-than-life canvases. Photorealism is a term used to describe paintings made from photographs. Photorealists use devices such as grids and projectors to copy the images from photographs onto canvases.

## Close, Up Close and Far Away

In 1989, Close suffered a stroke, which left him paralyzed from the neck down. After regaining movement in his arms (but not his hands), he was able to paint by attaching brushes to a special brace strapped to his arm. Without the use of his hands, he could no longer copy every detail in every square of the grid. Instead, he painted loose, colorful circles and dots in each square. Up close, these dots and blobs are completely abstract. But when you step back from one of these paintings, a person's face appears—and it can be startlingly realistic.

## Unknown Faces

When Chuck Close began his series of portraits, he used mostly his friends as subjects, many of whom were also artists. Originally, he wanted his paintings to picture relatively unknown people. Interestingly enough, the artists in his portraits achieved success in their own careers, so his paintings are no longer of anonymous people, but of world-renowned art stars.

Chuck Close, *Kiki*, 1993. Oil on canvas, 100 x 84⅛ in.

### Chuck Close, the Genius of the Grid

The first portraits painted by Chuck Close (b. 1940) were completely realistic and incredibly detailed, down to the last hair and freckle. To create these paintings, he took a picture of himself or a friend, drew a grid on top of it, and then copied every square onto a gigantic canvas. The size and detail of his nine-foot-tall faces make them impossible to ignore, and almost frightening. They practically command you to look at them. Normally, when we look at another person, we see their eyes, their hair, and maybe a few other features of their face. Seeing that same face towering nine feet above us is a completely different experience.

## Materials

You will need the following materials (in addition to your kit's paints, brushes, canvas with a grid already printed on it, transparent grid, palette, and palette knife):

- Tape (masking tape or clear tape)
- Paper towels
- Jar for water
- Spray bottle
- Camera
- Pencil

# Painting a Portrait with a Grid

Create a stunning portrait the same way Chuck Close does. The grid technique makes it easy to draw all the detail found in a photograph.

## 1 The Photograph

The first thing you will need to do is take a photograph of yourself or a friend. You can take a picture of yourself by holding your camera at arm's length, or, if your camera is equipped with a timer, you can set it up on a table or a tripod.

Be sure to set the camera at a distance that will frame your face in the photo. For this exercise, you don't want to have a lot of background information in your composition.

*This view is too close up.*

*This photo is poorly cropped.*

## 2 The Grid

If you are using a digital camera, print a copy of the photograph that is the right size for the large grid in your kit, 8½ x 11 inches. If you are using a 4 x 6 photograph, you can use the small grid from your kit.

Place the clear grid on top of your photograph, making sure that the edges of the image are in line with the edges of the grid, and tape them together.

|   | 1 | 2 | 3 | 4 | 5 | 6 | 7 | 8 | 9 | 1 |
|---|---|---|---|---|---|---|---|---|---|---|
| A |   |   |   |   |   |   |   |   |   |   |
| B |   |   |   |   |   |   |   |   |   |   |
| C |   |   |   |   |   |   |   |   |   |   |
| D |   |   |   |   |   |   |   |   |   |   |
| E |   |   |   |   |   |   |   |   |   |   |
| F |   |   |   |   |   |   |   |   |   |   |
| G |   |   |   |   |   |   |   |   |   |   |
| H |   |   |   |   |   |   |   |   |   |   |
| I |   |   |   |   |   |   |   |   |   |   |
| J |   |   |   |   |   |   |   |   |   |   |
| K |   |   |   |   |   |   |   |   |   |   |
| L |   |   |   |   |   |   |   |   |   |   |
| M |   |   |   |   |   |   |   |   |   |   |
| N |   |   |   |   |   |   |   |   |   |   |
| O |   |   |   |   |   |   |   |   |   |   |
| P |   |   |   |   |   |   |   |   |   |   |
| Q |   |   |   |   |   |   |   |   |   |   |
| R |   |   |   |   |   |   |   |   |   |   |
| S |   |   |   |   |   |   |   |   |   |   |
| T |   |   |   |   |   |   |   |   |   |   |
| U |   |   |   |   |   |   |   |   |   |   |

# 3  Drawing on the Canvas

In your kit, you will find a canvas that has a grid printed on it. Make a pencil sketch of each square in the photograph. In our example, we have sketched onto the canvas the squares in rows B and C and columns 7 and 8.

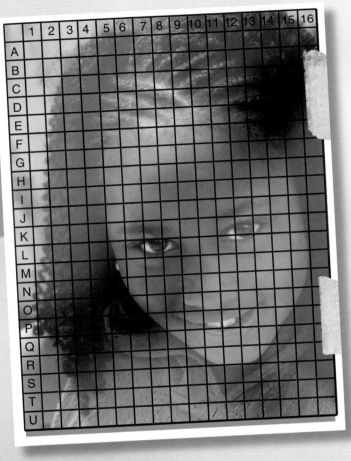

To make the features in your painting match those on your real face, go back to each individual square and analyze its proportions, thinking in terms of intersections, lines, diagonals, and curves.

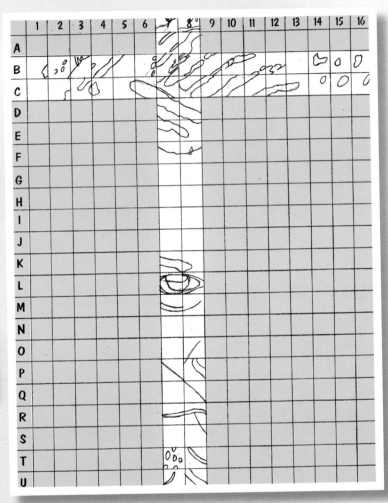

*Begin sketching each square onto your canvas.*

## TROUBLESHOOTING: PROPORTIONS

As you proceed square by square, your drawing should begin to look just like your subject. If it doesn't, it may be because your proportions are off. To correct this, go back to the grid and analyze the shapes within each square.

Look at the places where a shape intersects the edge of a square. Is the intersection halfway along the edge of the square, or a quarter of the way? Do any lines intersect the corners of the square? Are there any diagonals or curves within the square?

*Curved shape meets side of square a third of the way across.*

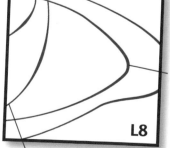

*Line curves back halfway up this side.*

*Curved shape intersects at a third of the way up.*

26

*The original photo*

## TROUBLESHOOTING: FACIAL FEATURES

The actual shapes of our features are often very different from how we remember them (or see them in drawings). Try to think of the details on your face as miscellaneous shapes, without classifying them as "lips," "eyes," or "hair."

*A common "cartoony" way to draw an eye*

*The eye as it actually appears*

*The line drawing—created one square at a time—is complete.*

## Hairy Challenge

Drawing hair can be a challenge. Even though hair is made up of thousands of tiny strands, that isn't the best way to paint it. To paint hair, think about the whole head of hair as a large shape that responds to light and shadow just like a feature on the face. Use blocks of color to describe hair, and avoid painting every strand of hair. One trick to help you do this is to squint your eyes when you look at the hair in the photograph. Can you see it as one large shape?

## 4 *Painting*

When your drawing is complete and you have sketched and refined every square, you can move into painting. Begin by working with colors as we did in the landscape exercise. What colors do you see in the photograph?

### Mixing Skin Tones

The color of skin varies widely from person to person. What color is your skin? It might be brown like coffee, yellow-pink like frosting, or orange-pink like a seashell. Notice also that there are light areas and dark areas on your face. This can be the result of light and shadow, or from variations in your complexion. Are there some areas on your face that are redder? Lighter? Cooler or warmer?

To mix skin colors for your portrait, you can use one of these "recipes" for different complexions.

Each category has recipes for the shadows and lighter areas of skin.

And then, because people come in infinite shades, you can create more of your own skin tone recipes.

## Pale complexion:

 A big dot of white, a small dot of yellow, a speck of red, and a speck of brown

**Shadow areas:** A medium dot of white, a small dot of yellow, a tiny dot of red, and two specks of blue

**Light areas:** Two big dots of white, a small dot of yellow, a speck of red, and a speck of brown

## Mid-brown complexion:

 A big dot of brown, a small dot of yellow, and a small dot of red

**Shadow areas:** A big dot of brown, a small dot of yellow, a small dot of red, and a small dot of blue

**Light areas:** A big dot of white, a small dot of brown, a small dot of yellow, and a speck of red

## Olive complexion:

 A small dot of white, a small dot of yellow, and a small dot of brown

**Shadow areas:** A small dot of yellow, a small dot of brown, a speck of red, and a speck of blue

**Light areas:** Two small dots of white, a small dot of yellow, and a small dot of brown

29

## 5 Finishing Touches

Imagine that each square is a small landscape all on its own. Mix colors for hair and skin, background, shadows, and light areas.

Fill each square with colors.

Close-up view of part of the painting

Paint the squares in completely.

# The Finished Portrait

## Painting Secrets:
## Cover the Whole Canvas First

Painters know that it is important to cover the entire canvas with paint before fine-tuning any area of the painting. Keeping this in mind can save you lots of trouble.

When you get paint on every part of the canvas, somehow the whole thing looks better, and you have a context for evaluating what you are doing. Areas that seemed like problems at first often look fine when the whole canvas is touched with paint.

If you are having trouble in any particular area, sometimes the best advice is to move on. Come back to it later—you may be surprised at what happens.

## More Portrait Projects to Try:

- Movie stars (look in magazines for photos)
- Your own baby pictures
- Statues
- Pets

# Other Approaches to Portraits

There are many other ways to approach painting a portrait. Here are some examples, featuring techniques that range from loose and casual-looking to very precise and realistic.

Sandra Power, *Artist with Red Flowers*, 2002.
Oil on canvas, 20 x 16 in.

Pirjo Berg, Untitled, 2000.
Oil on canvas, 14 x 11 in.

This realistic portrait gives an accurate likeness painted with loose brushstrokes. Berg's work ranges from this breezy and colorful style to a starkly simplified approach.

Although at first glance this painting looks like a still life of some flowers, it is actually a self-portrait. There is a mirror behind the pot of flowers, and in it we see a reflection of the artist painting. Even though we do not see her face, this painting says more about the artist than any direct representation of her face could, because it shows us what she loves to do.

Carole D'Inverno, Untitled, 2003.
Oil on canvas, 20 x 20 in.

This portrait is painted from the artist's imagination. The artist uses smooth brushstrokes and soft colors to give her paintings a dreamy appearance.

Aaron Power, *Boornaade*, 2003.
Oil on canvas, 24 x 24 in.

Aaron Power paints portraits of people he encountered on a trip to Africa with the Peace Corps. His paintings show the beauty of the countryside and its people and are good examples of painting's power to communicate between cultures.

# Abstract Paintings

Realistic paintings are windows to the world outside. The most realistic still life paintings make it appear as if you could reach into them and pick up the objects inside. Abstract paintings are more like windows into the mind of the artist, describing thoughts, feelings, and ideas without using any objects.

After hundreds of years of painters trying to perfect the illusion of realistic painting, modern artists decided to do things differently. Contemporary painters wanted their paintings to be solid surfaces, not "open windows." One of the ways they achieved this was to avoid including any recognizable imagery in their paintings, because images that are recognizable can make the painting look like a window into space. They used color and shapes, but not shapes that looked like objects or pictures of things.

Strong abstract paintings are able to make people think and feel, and they do this without using pictures or words. By leaving out the pictures of objects and recognizable, nameable stuff, abstract paintings give more room for viewers to interpret what they are seeing.

Helen Frankenthaler, *Acres*, 1959. Oil on canvas, 93 x 93¾ in.

## Helen Frankenthaler, Painter of the Inner World

One painter who brought an innovative technique to abstract painting was Helen Frankenthaler (b. 1928). In her technique, called *staining*, paint is diluted to a liquid form (by adding turpentine to oil paint or water to acrylic paint) and poured onto the canvas. When liquid paint is allowed to flow freely across the surface of the canvas, it creates unpredictable, free-form shapes that a brush or a palette knife could never make. Her paintings are windows into the world inside all of us.

## Materials

You will need the following materials (in addition to your kit's paints, brushes, canvas, palette, and palette knife):

- Small plastic containers (yogurt cups with lids are perfect for mixing and storing paint)
- Newspaper to protect the table from spills and runoff
- Jar for water
- Paper towels
- Spray bottle

# Making Your Own Abstract Painting

Use Helen Frankenthaler's staining technique (or invent your own) to make a powerful piece of abstract art

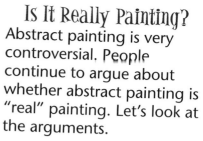

## 1 Thinking Abstractly

In the last three exercises, the subject matter was real and specific. In abstract paintings, the subject matter is not so well defined. Abstract paintings can be about many things, including color, paint, emotion, experience, ideas, and the natural world. That's a lot to choose from!

For this exercise, let's narrow the subject matter down and do a painting about stormy weather. You can think about this topic in a number of ways. To get started, ask yourself some questions:

- *Do you have a memory of a storm, or of particularly intense weather? This could include beautiful weather as well as thunder, lightning, and rain.*

- *How does an approaching storm look?*

- *What are a storm's colors?*

Think of some other ways to interpret the subject "stormy weather." How about an argument, or fireworks in the sky? Or hats blowing off, leaves swirling, or umbrellas turning inside out? Maybe the storm was so strong it made its own painting by blowing all of your paint containers over.

What feelings or emotions can you associate with the storm? Do you feel happy, sad, or scared? What color would these emotions have? For instance, you might represent anger with the color red, insecurity with orange, or the joy of splashing in puddles with blue.

## 2 Mixing Fluid Paint

Think about what color or colors you want to use in your painting. Squeeze three big dots of each color into individual yogurt cups. Pour three tablespoons of water into each cup, enough to cover the paint. Replace the lids and shake well.

The result should be paint that is runny enough to pour, like soup, but not so runny that it looks more like water than paint.

*Paint and water (left cup) and mixed paint (right cup)*

# 3  *Experimenting with Paint*

Start your painting by covering large areas of the paper with diluted color.

First, get the canvas wet by spraying it lightly with your spray bottle.

Next, think about what colors you want to use in the painting. In our example, the background is mainly blue, with a little bit of red.

Using your ½-inch flat brush, spread some of the background color onto the canvas. You may need to dilute your colors a little more to get them to spread evenly.

While the surface is still wet, experiment with pouring some other colors into the blue field. What does the paint do when you dribble it onto a wet surface? How is this different from the other exercises, when you worked with a dry surface and thicker paint?

*Thin paint spread over a wet canvas*

*Thin paint poured on a wet surface*

*Thick paint dribbled on a wet surface*

*Puddles of color next to each other*

## *Get Experimental*

In many abstract paintings, the artist is experimenting with paint and showing how paint behaves in different circumstances. Can you think of new ways to use your paints?

- Pour diluted paint onto a wet surface.

- Dribble thick fluid paint onto a wet surface.

- Place two puddles of color next to each other with their edges touching and watch the pigments swirl into each other, mixing by themselves.

*The painting so far, after experimenting with the staining technique*

Paint is made of tiny particles of color called *pigment*. A fully loaded brush is concentrated with pigment particles. When the brush touches the water on the surface of a wet piece of paper, the pigment rushes out of the brush, spreading quickly in dramatic patterns.

## Painting Secrets: Wet-in-Wet

Painting with a brush full of fluid paint on a wet piece of paper is a technique called *wet-in-wet*. This technique produces dramatic effects that are perfect for representing the sky, clouds, and weather—as well as emotions!

Virginia Howlett, *Pruth Bay*, 1992.
Watercolor on paper, 22 x 30 in.

## Things to Try with a Dry Surface:

At some point in your process, allow the paint on your canvas to dry. By working on top of dry paint, you can achieve a variety of effects that are not possible on a wet surface.

1. Scrub paint onto the canvas with a brush.

2. Make delicate lines with the side of your palette knife.

3. Squeeze paint from the tube onto your canvas and smear it with your palette knife.

*Dry surface effects*

# 4 Finishing Your Painting

After experimenting with some wet and dry painting techniques, sit back and consider whether your piece is finished.

There are a few guidelines to consider when deciding whether to continue painting or to stop.

1. Generally, it is a good idea to cover most of the canvas, spreading the painting out to one or more of the edges.

2. Blank areas of canvas can be a good thing. The areas of your painting with less paint coverage show off your brushwork. Active brushwork makes your painting look spontaneous, as though you had a thought that just sprang out of your mind and onto the paper effortlessly.

3. There is a chance you could overwork the painting. Overworking the colors can lead to what artists call "mud." This happens when the colors you wanted to keep distinct and bright mix together to form a soupy, brown mess. Mud might be appropriate for some things, like your stormy weather painting, but sometimes it just doesn't look right.

*"Mud" can ruin your painting.*

4. You might want to let your painting dry for some time before deciding it's done. If you aren't sure, it's a good idea to leave the room and go do something else for a while. When you return to the painting, you might have a better idea of what to do.

## The Finished Abstract Painting

When it comes to abstract paintings, the world is wide open. Any subject matter, inspiration, or technique can lead to an amazing piece of abstract art.

## More Abstract Projects to Try:

- Paint a picture with your "wrong" hand (if you're left-handed, paint with your right hand; if you're right-handed, paint with your left).
- Instead of brushes, try painting with forks, leaves, old shoelaces, or sponges.
- Create a work of abstraction about a certain day: for example, tomorrow, Halloween, or your first day of school.

Stephanie Dennis, *Turquoise*, 2003.
Oil on canvas, 66 x 59½ in.

Joanne Pavlak, Untitled, 2004.
Oil on canvas, 8¼ x 8¼ in.

Andrée Carter, *Big Red*, 2004.
Oil and resin on board, 30 x 30 in.

This painting has a light, airy feeling like the summer sky. The artist builds up layers of light color, which makes the painting shimmer. The dark band on the bottom edge of the painting suggests that it is a landscape, but the light shapes on the top look like something else. What do you see in the painting? What do the colors make you feel?

This artist, like Helen Frankenthaler, is inspired by nature. Although her paintings don't show anything in particular in the environment, their color and texture suggest a natural origin. Does the thick, textured green make you think of something in nature? Your backyard? A forest?

Some abstract painters explore different qualities of color in their work. This painting by Andrée Carter is all about the color red. She covers the canvas with many bold shades of red and accentuates that color by adding bits of green, red's complement on the color wheel.

Patricia Hagen, *Onset*, 2003.
Mixed media, 11 x 14 in.

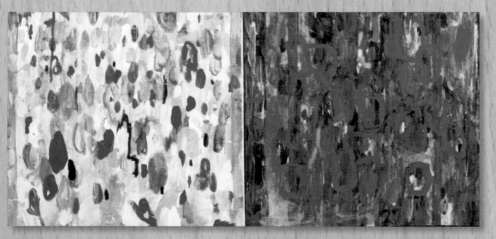

Randy McCoy, Untitled, 2003.
Oil on canvas, 30 x 60 in.

In this abstract piece, the painter has left the subject out and focused on the beauty and colors of the background. The pools of color look like bubbles of thought floating up on a screen, giving a lighthearted feeling. Does this piece inspire you? Does it make you feel anything in particular?

The imagined forms in Patricia Hagen's paintings have a biological feel, like something seen under a microscope. The shapes she uses *almost* look like real objects, but are indefinite enough to be abstract. The shapes seem to float in the white background, like small animals in a pond.

# The History of Painting

The history of painting is written as artists develop new methods, their materials improve, and the ideas behind paintings evolve. Painting is constantly growing and changing. Who knows what chapter you could add to the story of painting?

## Around 25,000 BC

## Around 600 BC

## 1400s & 1500s

Leonardo da Vinci, *Mona Lisa*, 1503–1506. Oil on wood, 77 x 53 cm. Louvre, Paris, France.

## 1839

### The Beginning

The history of painting begins with the earliest known paintings, the cave paintings of Europe. Prehistoric artists used paint from charred wood and vegetable dyes, spitting the pigments through reeds and rubbing it onto cave walls to make paintings that would last thousands of years.

### Ancient Innovations

Artists in ancient Greece made paintings by applying black glazes onto vases. This "black-figure" style featured illustrations of stories from Greek mythology. But even back then, painters were always looking for new ways to make art. In 530 BC, artists created a new technique and the innovative "red-figure" style became very popular.

### Capturing It Perfectly

Realistic painting reached its peak during the Renaissance (REN-uh-sonce), a period when art, culture, and ideas flourished in Europe. Some of the paintings created during this time are so well known that we refer to the artists by their first names. Leonardo, Michelangelo, and Raphael are some of the most famous "first name" Renaissance painters.

### Photography Is Here

Because the camera could take pictures that imitated reality flawlessly, a group of painters who called themselves Impressionists developed a new way of painting. Impressionist paintings were loose and free, and captured the beauty the painters saw in the world. The Impressionists and other painters no longer felt the need to create realistic paintings.

## 1841

## 1910

Pablo Picasso, *Portrait of Dora Maar*, 1937.
Oil on canvas, 92 x 65 cm.
Musée Picasso, Paris, France.

## 1947

Jackson Pollock, *Watery Paths*, 1947.
Oil on canvas. Galleria Nazionale d'Arte Moderna,
Rome, Italy.

## 1970s

Chuck Close, *Robert/104,072*, 1973–74. Synthetic polymer paint and ink with graphite on gessoed canvas, 108 x 84 in. Gift of J. Frederic Byers III and promised gift of an anonymous donor (286.1976), The Museum of Modern Art, New York, NY, USA, photo: Digital Image © The Museum of Modern Art / Licensed by Scala / Art Resource, NY.

## Tubes Change Everything

The American painter John Rand invented light metal paint tubes in 1841. A year later, a company started selling paints in tubes. Painters were finally able to carry oil paints into the countryside and paint outside. This enabled Monet and other Impressionist painters to capture the vibrant colors seen in the sunlight. The painter Pierre-Auguste Renoir later said that "without paints in tubes, there would have been no Cezanne, no Monet . . . . nothing of what the journalists were later to call Impressionism."

## What the Mind Sees

Pablo Picasso and the Cubists developed a new style of painting to express the idea that the mind can "see" things from many sides at once. A Cubist portrait painting would show strangely mixed views of facial features: the nose seen from the side, an eye seen from the front, and the mouth open on one side and closed on the other. Painting was moving even further away from realistic depictions of the world.

## No More Brushes!

Jackson Pollock grew tired of depicting realistic imagery in his paintings, and then he grew tired of using brushes. He began throwing and dripping paint onto his canvases in 1947, and made a huge impression on the art world. He was known to dump paint from atop a ladder onto a canvas placed on the floor.

## Back to Reality

After centuries of painters reacting against realism and painting abstract images, Chuck Close brought everything full circle by painting incredibly realistic portraits. Instead of battling the camera, he embraced photography. Before he turned to his intricate grid portraits, Close created incredibly realistic paintings.

# Glossary

**Abstract**
A painting or other work of art that uses colors and free-form shapes instead of depictions of actual people and things.

**Color wheel**
A special arrangement of colors that shows the different ways they are related to each other.

**Complementary colors**
Colors that sit directly opposite each other on the color wheel.

**Cool colors**
Blue and other colors that contain a lot of blue.

**Cubism**
A style of painting from the early 1900s that used abstract forms and showed different views of something simultaneously.

**Gesso**
A substance spread on a canvas to prepare it for painting. Also called *sizing*.

**Impressionism**
A style of painting from the late 1800s and early 1900s that used colorful strokes and dabs of paint to capture light and the natural world.

**Landscape**
A painting or other work of art that depicts a scene from the natural world.

**Neutrals**
A group of colors made by mixing two complementary colors. Grays, browns, and earth tones are neutrals.

**Palette**
A surface used for mixing and keeping paints while painting.

**Palette knife**
A tool used for mixing paints, applying paint to a canvas, or making marks in paint.

**Pigment**
A powdery substance that comes from gemstones, rocks, or other materials. A pigment gives paint its color.

**Primary colors**
Colors that cannot be created by mixing other colors, also called *foundation colors*. Red, yellow, and blue are the primary colors.

**Realism**
A style of painting that tries to create very lifelike depictions of people and objects.

**Secondary colors**
Colors made by mixing two primary colors. Orange, purple, and green are the secondary colors.

**Shade**
A color made by adding black to another color.

**Still life**
A painting or other work of art that depicts a collection of objects, often arranged by the artist.

**Tertiary colors**
Colors made by mixing a primary color and a neighboring secondary color. Red-orange, yellow-orange, yellow-green, blue-green, blue-violet, and red-violet are the tertiary colors.

**Tint**
A color made by adding white to another color.

**Warm colors**
Colors on the opposite side of the color wheel from the cool colors. Red, yellow, orange, and red-violet are all warm colors.